One Tiger GROWLS

A Counting Book of Animal Sounds

Ginger Wadsworth • Illustrated by James M. Needham

Charlesbridge

*To Adrian, nephew . . . Dodger fan . . . storyteller
And to the Bruen family, for making
African animal noises in the night
—G. W.*

*For Charlene, forever and always
—J. N.*

One tiger growls *gr-r-r-r-r*.

1

During the heat of the day, tigers rest in the shade. Sometimes they lie in streams or shallow pools of water to keep cool. These large cats begin to hunt for food at dusk. Because of their stripes, tigers are hard to spot among the trees and grasses. They usually hunt and live alone. When they meet, tigers might greet each other by rubbing their heads together and growling *gr-r-r-r-r*.

2

Two red roosters crow *cock-a-doodle-do*.

These male chickens like to wake up early. Before sunrise they strut about, shaking the combs on top of their heads. Roosters often jump to a high spot—a fence post, the roof of a barn, or the wheel of a tractor. They fluff their feathers and stretch their necks. Then they crow *cock-a-doodle-do* over and over again to announce the start of a new day.

3 Three burros bray *hee-haw-hee-haw*.

Burros live in the dry parts of the world and can go without water for several days. They are much smaller than horses and have long pointed ears that stick out. Burros trot up and down steep hills on their tough, U-shaped hooves without slipping or falling. They will eat twigs, leaves, and thistles, but they like grass the best! When they see other burros, they bray *hee-haw-hee-haw*.

4 Great horned owls sleep during the day and wake up at night. Sometimes these large birds flap silently across the sky on their broad, rounded wings to hunt. Owls catch small animals and birds in their sharp talons. They fly to a treetop or cliff ledge and tear their food into bite-sized pieces with their beaks. Other times great horned owls perch in trees and hoot *hoo-hoo-hoo-hoo* until dawn.

5

Five kittens mew *meow-meow.*

Kittens are helpless at birth, but they grow quickly.
After about ten days, they open their eyes and start
to grow tiny teeth. Kittens spend hours washing their
fur, using their paws and tongues like washcloths.
They even clean their brothers and sisters, too!
Kittens need lots of sleep, but when they wake up,
they mew *meow-meow* for their mother's milk.

Six woodpeckers drum *rat-a-tat-tat.*

6

All day long woodpeckers look for bugs that live in trees. Some woodpeckers peel off pieces of bark. Others tap on trees with their chisel-shaped bills and hammer little holes in the wood. With their long sticky tongues they pull out grubs and insects to eat. Then the woodpeckers move to other trees and drum *rat-a-tat-tat* all over again.

7

Seven gorillas grunt *wuh-wuh-wuh-wuh!*

A group of gorillas moves through the thick forest. Gorillas often stop and sit, reaching out with their long arms for plants to eat. Mothers feed their babies. Sometimes a male gorilla stands and thumps his chest. He grunts *wuh-wuh-wuh-wuh* to show off. He throws leaves and roots, and the young gorillas copy him. At night gorillas make leafy nests on the ground and go to sleep.

8

Eight coyotes yowl *yip-yip-yip*.

Coyotes have tan coats mixed with hairs of rusty brown and gray. This helps them to hide in grasses, rocks, and brush. They use their sharp eyesight, good hearing, and strong sense of smell to hunt. They can trot long distances to find food. When evening comes, they point their muzzles to the sky and "sing." They yowl *yip-yip-yip*, and a chorus of songs echoes across the land.

Nine squirrels chatter *chitter-chitter-chitter.*

9

These bushy-tailed animals scamper across the ground. They dig holes and hide nuts. Sometimes they race around with other squirrels, or they stand on their hind feet and check for enemies, such as hawks, foxes, coyotes, and weasels. In case of danger, squirrels leap up a tree trunk and hide in the leaves. They flick their tails and angrily chatter *chitter-chitter-chitter.*

Ten hippos bellow *un-n-nk, un-n-nk.*

10

Hippopotamuses are huge! They can weigh five to eight thousand pounds. They like to feel light by floating in a lake or river. Hippos stick out their big heads to breathe and grunt *un-n-nk, un-n-nk.* They look around with their bulging eyes. If hippos open their huge mouths to yawn, they show off their pink gums and pointed tusks. When they wiggle their ears, they send droplets of water flying.

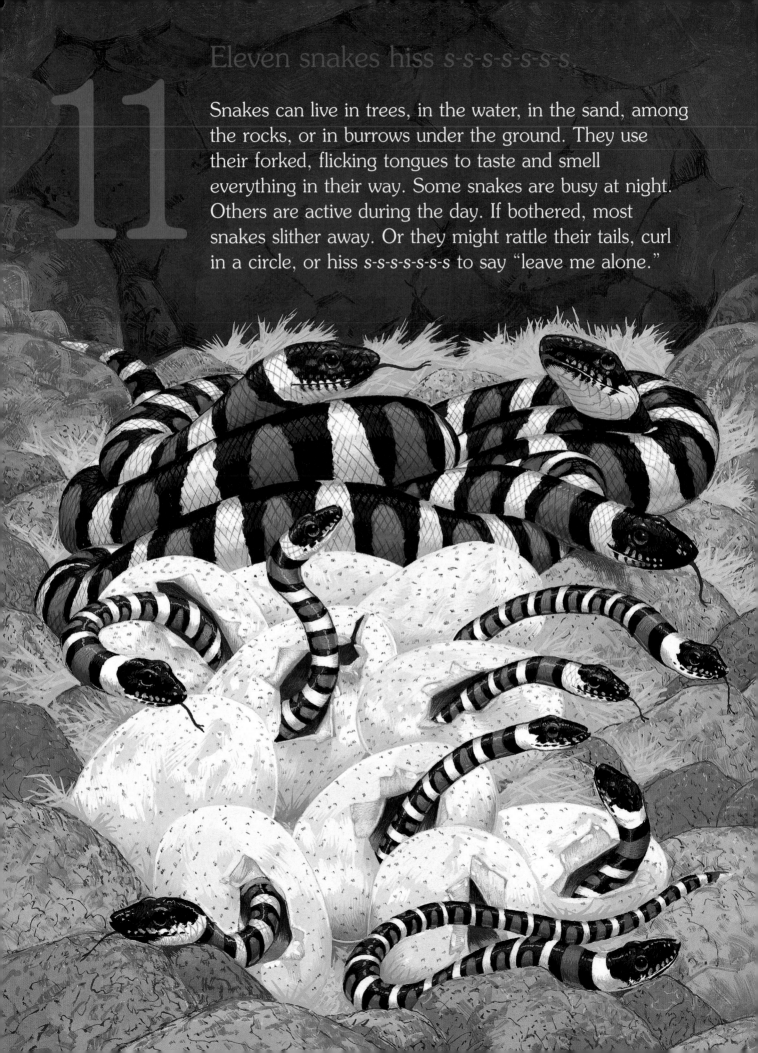

11

Snakes can live in trees, in the water, in the sand, among the rocks, or in burrows under the ground. They use their forked, flicking tongues to taste and smell everything in their way. Some snakes are busy at night. Others are active during the day. If bothered, most snakes slither away. Or they might rattle their tails, curl in a circle, or hiss s-s-s-s-s-s-s to say "leave me alone."

Twelve sea lions bark *ork-ork-ork*.

12

Sea lions live in the ocean near the rocky coasts. Using their flippers, they dive deep in the water to find fish and squid to eat. Some of the time, large groups of sea lions come ashore to sleep in the sun. They use one another as big soft pillows. Later they bark *ork-ork-ork* while they play games with other sea lions in the ocean.

Thirteen mice squeal
squeak-squeak-squeak.

These small rodents scurry about, using their long whiskers to feel the way. Mice squeal *squeak-squeak-squeak* as they look for a warm place to build a nest—under the ground, in a pile of leaves, in an old bird's nest, in a house, even in a coat pocket! They have dark round eyes and big front teeth that never stop growing. Mice chew wood and walls as well as seeds and grasses to trim their teeth.

Fourteen llamas hum
um-m-m-m-m-m.

14

Llamas are members of the camel family. They have long necks, soft hooves, and woolly coats. Wild llamas live in herds in the mountains of South America. Trained llamas are used as pack animals around the world. They are surefooted, smart, and have good memories. When llamas are angry, they might spit! But if they are happy, they often hum *um-m-m-m-m.*

15

Fifteen gulls shriek *ke-yah, ke-yah*.

Gulls are always hungry. That is why they make great garbage collectors! They help keep our beaches and our parks clean. Waddling across the sand on their webbed feet, they eat dead birds and fish. They finish sandwiches and apple cores on school playgrounds. As the gulls circle in the sky to hunt for food, they shriek *ke-yah, ke-yah* to one another.

16 Sixteen long-horned grasshoppers chirp *katydid-katydidn't*.

Long-horned grasshoppers are also called katydids. At night during the summer and fall, katydids rub their front wings together, chirping their *katydid-katydidn't* call. These six-legged insects are hard to see because their green wings look like leaves. They feel their way along twigs with their long antennae, or horns. Or they jump from branch to branch on their strong hind legs to find other insects to eat.

Seventeen
killer whales blow *whoosh-whoosh*.

17

With their torpedo-shaped bodies, killer whales can speed through the water. They also like to leap out of the water and crash back down, making a big splash! Killer whales breathe air through a blowhole—a kind of nostril—on top of their heads. After closing the blowhole, they can stay under water for up to fifteen minutes. Then the whales must float to the surface and blow *whoosh-whoosh* to get rid of the used air.

Eighteen crows cackle *caw-caw-caw*.

Crows are found along rivers and streams, in the woods, near orchards, and even in city parks. They build bowl-shaped nests in trees, sharing the area with other crows. When another bird, a stranger, or a large animal comes near, these shiny black birds cackle *caw-caw-caw* to try to scare away their enemies. Crows can also sing soft songs and imitate other birds and animals.

Nineteen spotted hyenas laugh
hee-hee-hee-hee-hee.

19

Hyenas look like large dogs, even though they are not related to them. They use their sharp eyes and ears to help them find food at night. A pack of hyenas can run for miles across the African plain hunting a wildebeest, zebra, or other big animal. They bark, snarl, growl, and laugh *hee-hee-hee-hee-hee* while they eat. That is why they are called laughing hyenas.

20

Twenty frogs croak *ribbit-ribbit*.

Frogs are great jumpers. They leap into the water and swim easily, using their webbed feet like flippers. While they float on top of the water, the males croak *ribbit-ribbit* to attract the female frogs. With their big bulging eyes, they watch for tasty insects, spiders, and baby water snakes to grab in their wide grinning mouths.

Text copyright © 1999 by Ginger Wadsworth
Illustrations copyright © 1999 by Charlesbridge Publishing

Published by Charlesbridge Publishing
85 Main Street, Watertown, MA 02472
(617) 926-0329
www.charlesbridge.com

Printed in the United States of America
(hc) 10 9 8 7 6 5 4 3 2 1
(sc) 10 9 8 7 6 5 4 3 2 1

Library of Congress Cataloging-in-Publication Data
Wadsworth, Ginger.
One tiger growls: a counting book of animal sounds/Ginger Wadsworth;
illustrated by James M. Needham.
p.   cm.
Summary: Briefly describes the behavior of and sounds made by various animals,
from one growling tiger to twenty croaking frogs.
ISBN 0-88106-273-1 (reinforced for library use)
ISBN 0-88106-274-X (softcover)
1. Counting—Juvenile literature. 2. Animal sounds—Juvenile literature.
3. Animal behavior—Juvenile literature. [1. Animal sounds.
2. Animals—Habits and behavior. 3. Counting.]
I. Needham, James, ill. II. Title.
QA113.W32   1999
513.2'11
[E]—DC21   97-37050

The illustrations in this book are done in gouache on Crescent illustration board.
The display type and text type were set in Souvenir, Zorba, and Flare.
Color separations were made by Eastern Rainbow, Derry, New Hampshire.
Printed and bound by Worzalla Publishing Company, Stevens Point, Wisconsin
Production supervision by Brian G. Walker
Designed by Diane M. Earley
This book was printed on recycled paper.